JOAN STEINER

LOOK-ALIKES™

Photography by Thomas Lindley

LB
1837

LITTLE, BROWN AND COMPANY

Boston   New York   Toronto   London

For George, Holly, Derek, and George C.

First Edition

Library of Congress Cataloging-in-Publication Data

Steiner, Joan (Joan Catherine)
    Look-Alikes ™/ Joan Steiner ; photography by Thomas Lindley. — 1st ed.
        p.   cm.
    Summary: Simple verses challenge readers to identify the everyday
objects used to construct eleven three-dimensional scenes in Look-Alike Land.
    ISBN 0-316-81255-2
    1. Picture puzzles — Juvenile literature.   [1. Picture puzzles.]
1. Title.
    GV1507.P47574   1998
    793.73 — dc21   97-32795

10 9 8 7 6 5 4 3 2

SC

Published simultaneously in Canada by Little, Brown & Company (Canada) Limited

Printed in Hong Kong

The illustrations in this book are photographs of three-dimensional collages created from
found objects. The text was set in Xavier Sans Medium Condensed.
The display type is Hoffman Black Titling.

Where do peanuts look like teddy bears
Or the carousel horses you ride at fairs?
In Look-Alike Land! That magical spot
Where everyday things look like what they're not.
A balloon is a dress? Pistachios are flowers?
Look-alikes can keep you looking for hours.
More than one hundred objects in each scene (but two)—
Find some or ALL. It's up to you.
(For you puzzle hounds who like to keep track,
A complete list of look-alikes appears at the back.)

So come with me—I'll be your guide
To all the wonders you'll see inside....

Come along! Jump aboard! Grab hold of my hand.
We're crossing the border into Look-Alike Land.
Everything's changing! Believe it or not,
It looks like this engine's a huge COFFEEPOT!

Our long trip is over. The train's in the station.
It's time to use your imagination!
Start searching for look-alikes right in this tunnel.
See the top of the newsstand? It looks like a FUNNEL.

Out of the station and into the light,
Look-Alike City's a magical sight!
And the look-alikes keep getting better and better.
I see a building that looks like a SWEATER.

While we're in town, let's stop at the store.
It's packed with look-alikes from ceiling to floor.
A RAZOR that vacuums is really quite handy,
Or how 'bout a lamp that looks like MINT CANDY?

We'll start our tour with the park and the zoo.
Let's search for look-alikes while strolling through.
Here's one that isn't often seen—
A sandbox that looks like a TAMBOURINE.

I'm so excited! Look-Alike Fair is in town!
It's a great place to go when the sun's going down.
Look-alikes spinning — twirlers, whirlers, and whizzers,
And a huge Ferris wheel that looks just like SCISSORS.

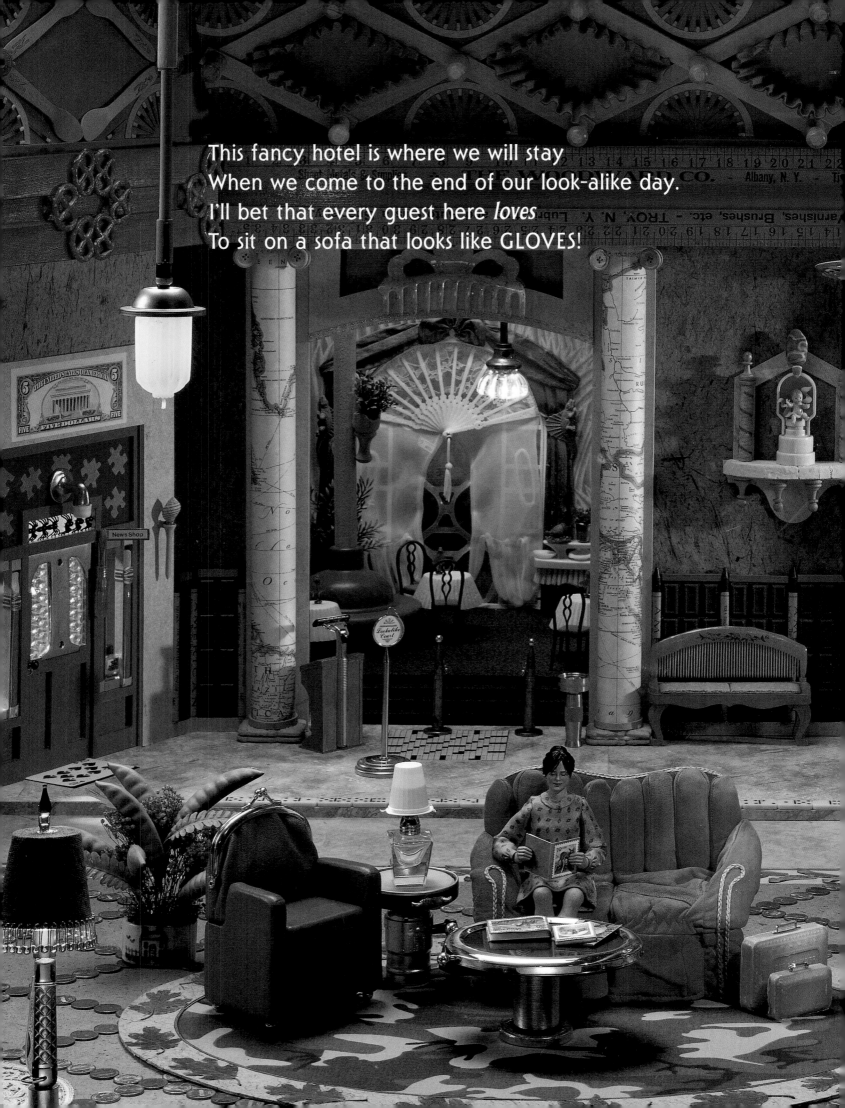

This fancy hotel is where we will stay
When we come to the end of our look-alike day.
I'll bet that every guest here *loves*
To sit on a sofa that looks like GLOVES!

Up bright and early, let's visit a street
Where the houses look good enough to eat.
And not *just* the houses, let it be said.
It looks like those people are walking on BREAD!

Say, are you hungry? Let's make a stop
For chocolate shakes at Stanley's Sweet Shop.
I see something here that really is funny.
Look up! That ceiling looks just like MONEY.

And now for an extra-special treat:
The Look-Alike Circus, front-row seat!
The clown is so funny, and his outfit's so quaint
With those pants that look like TUBES OF PAINT.

The time has come to sail away,
But please come back another day.
Down by the harbor, we'll say "Farewell!"
And ring you out on the big COW BELL.

EXTRA CHALLENGE

Let's scan every scene again
For *two* things that start with P-E-N.
One is something you can spend;
The other sharpens at the end.
On every page they can be found.
Did you spot them first time round?

HOW TO COUNT THE LOOK-ALIKES

1. If more than one of the same object is used to make up *one* look-alike (such as ten pencils making up a fence), it counts as *one* look-alike. But if the same or a similar object appears elsewhere in the scene to make a *different* look-alike (such as a pencil appearing as a flagpole), it counts again.

2. Miniatures don't count as look-alikes unless they appear as something different from a larger version of themselves. For example, a toy car that represents a real car is not a look-alike. But a toy car that looks like a fire hydrant *does* count.

3. As long as you can identify an object, you don't have to get the name exactly right.

THE LOOK-ALIKES

Asterisks indicate hard-to-find items — for super-sleuths only!

TRAIN

☛ *132 Look-Alikes*

LOCOMOTIVE: Front of engine: coffeepot, overalls buckle, bingo call number, nuts (nut-and-bolt type). **Cowcatcher:** toy truck, harmonica, nail clipper, red cocktail fork, package carrying handle, red birthday candle. **Lower engine and wheels:** cap guns, roll of film, battery, black ballpoint pen cap*, toy handcuffs, wristwatch face, toy compass, drafting compass with pencil, matchbook, can opener, green pencil-top eraser, wrenches, cat-food cans, bottle tops, (more bingo call numbers), spark plug, tire pressure gauge, die, small calculator, candy thermometer, hacksaw, pencil sharpener, buckle, bottle stopper, pencil, felt-tip marker, bouillon cubes. **Upper engine:** spool of thread, postage stamp, Slinky, sink plug, small jar of honey, knitting needle, green button, electrical connectors (holding knitting needle), sewing needles in paper. **Cab:** child's sandals, carpenter's clamp, pushpins, subway token, hinge, photographic slide, big safety pin, old-fashioned keys. **REST OF TRAIN: Coal carrier:** pocketbook, green padlock, two books, toy car, ballpoint pen refill, corkscrew/bottle opener, can/bottle opener, jar tops*, sewing machine bobbins. **Freight car:** cardboard box, steak knives, swizzle sticks, spiral notepads, rubber bands, balsa airplane parts, toy pilot's wings*, toothpick, wooden match, crochet hook, twist ties, price tag, orange ticket, tape measure, tiny plastic clothespin, small clasp envelopes, orange cocktail forks, theater ticket voucher, green comb, domino*, green alphabet letters, key holder, bulldog paper clips*, dollar bill. **Passenger car**: six-pack box, green toothbrush*, green pick-up stick, penny, six-inch ruler, paintbrush*, wristwatch band, half-dollars*, paper clip, carpenter's clamp*, razors (steps)*, ring, luggage tag*, toy wooden animal. **WATER TOWER:** Sifter, dollar bill, wooden cocktail forks, chopsticks, wire whisk, rubber stamp handle, needle and thread, weighted fishhook. TRACKS, OVERPASS, AND FOREGROUND: Screwdriver, TV antenna, chopstick*, cinnamon sticks, food grater*, twelve-inch ruler, jigsaw puzzle pieces, stapler, guitar case, pinecones, potatoes, pecans. **SMOKE AND SKY:** Cotton, white rose, toy bunny, baby bootie, pearl earring, baby tooth, jingle bell, button, acorn, seashell, pearl, snap.

TRAIN STATION

☞ 78 Look-Alikes

FOREGROUND AND CEILING: Keys, windshield wipers, dominoes, flashlight, kazoo, badminton racquets, embroidery hoops, hangers, scissors, clothespins, wooden fork, juicer. UPPER PLATFORM LEVEL: **Back wall**: paintbrushes, jingle bells, chopsticks, spring-type clothespins, silverware organizer trays, plastic spoon, spiral notepad, pocket calculator. **Snack bar**: toothbrushes, travel toothbrush holder, clear plastic ruler, artist's blending stick, paper clips, stamp*, pick-up stick, magnifying glass, sticks of gum*, high-heeled doll shoes*. **Ticket booth**: fever thermometers, pearl earrings, supermarket bonus stamps, dollar bills. **Waiting room**: vegetable steamer, egg slicer, cigarettes, nail clippers, hair clip, weighted fishhooks, small screwdriver. **Information booth**: baby-bottle nipple, white chess pawns. **Railing and gates**: drywall screws, binder clips, tape measure, black crayon. **LOWER PLATFORMS:** Disposable razors, pen nibs, funnel, matchbox. **Train**: lipstick, wallet, birthday candles, photographic slides, penny, retractable measuring tape, chocolate-covered marshmallow cookies, rubber faucet attachment, whistle, fondue fork, nut (nut-and-bolt type), thermos, shoe-polish tins, wrench, drafting compass with pencil, nine-volt battery, C battery. **Baggage cart**: matches, bingo call number, snaps, peanuts, die, cough drop in wrapper, Tootsie Roll, caramels, Scrabble tiles, eye (hook-and-eye type).

LOOK-ALIKE CITY

☞ 207 Look-Alikes

CANOPY: Garden rake, bullets, Christmas ornament. **BUILDINGS TO LEFT OF INTERSECTION**: **Building at far left**: felt-tip pen, drinking straw, old cookbook. **Building on left-hand corner**: green suitcase, mousetraps, pistachio nuts (red and natural), toy trumpet Christmas ornament, staple remover, pastels, honey dippers, recorders, handcuffs, cupcake papers, bottle cap, toothbrush-and-cup holder, X-Acto knives, pearl earrings, blue crayons, tube of paint, hook (hook-and-eye type)*, uninflated pink balloon, drill bit, travel soap dish with soap, pearl anklet, Smarties candy, spools of thread, roll of cap-gun caps, birthday-candle holder, sticks of gum*, whistle, price stickers, doll shoes, toy wooden geese, cap guns, nuts and bolts. **BUILDINGS AND THINGS SEEN THROUGH INTERSECTION**: **Bus**: carpenter's clamp, audiocassette, clear button*. **Building behind bus**: champagne cork, rubber stamp, Scrabble tile, baseball card*, paint stirring stick. **Blue-roofed building and behind it**: billiard cue chalk, matchboxes, phone jack, blue pencil-tip erasers, spiral notepad, posable sculptor's mannequin, saltshaker top, hourglass egg timers, ballpoint pen and holder, folding carpenter's ruler*, wafer cookies. **Church**: pen nibs, brown pencils, chocolate chips, metronome, chess king, wedding band*, penny, purse, small bottles, chess pawns, bobby pins*, file folders, newspaper, plastic cocktail forks, tape measure, buttons, pecans, breakfast cereal hexagons. **Truck**: packets of sewing needles. **In intersection**: punch-type can opener, M&M's, drafting compasses, pearls, small yellow pencils, fishing line weights, clothing label, small chalkboard, lentils. RESTAURANT BUILDING: Book, bell, chess bishops, paintbrushes, alphabet noodles, nutcracker, cable-knit sweater, black-eyed peas, fancy toothpicks, corn kernels, pushpins, pretzels, peanut, safety pins, clothespins, dog biscuits, price tags, dollar bills, matchbook, blue birthday candles, silver dollars (tables), electrical connectors (vases)*, champagne cork cages, paper clips, melba toasts. **Signpost on corner**: glass cutter. DELICATESSEN BUILDING: Supermarket bonus stamps, jigsaw puzzle piece, cigarillo, ruler, shade pull, dried maple-seed cases, saltines, chopsticks, incense sticks, gum erasers, wool label, postage stamps, paint-chip strip, emery board, miniature watercolor kits, Cheerios, plastic protractor, pet collar, tiny buckles, luggage tag, diamond ring, thimbles, candy corn, nail clippers, drop earring, candy in wrapper, pinecone, bingo game cards, alphabet blocks, yellow pencil sharpener, spool of red thread, die, TinkerToy part, red bouillon cube*, seashell, button*, swizzle stick, toy car. **Signposts in front of deli building**: machine screw, large nail, museum admission tag, digital watch face, bulldog paper clip, bread closure tag, screwdriver, nut (nut-and-bolt type). TOY SHOP BUILDING: Shutter, Scrabble board, knitting needles, cocktail forks, corncob holders, plastic bandage, red crayons, Chinese finger puzzle, hair clips, jack (from game of jacks), wooden matches, postage stamps, chess knight, barrettes, corn kernels, pistachio nut; spiral pasta, seashell, ball-headed pin, cork, model train freight car (Note: Puppet, teddy bear, and goose are miniatures rather than look-alikes.). **Hydrant**: roll of film, snaps, saltshaker top. **CAR**: Black shoe, mushrooms, sewing needle, zipper slide, acorn, silver barrettes, key-chain clasp (door handle)*. **FOREGROUND AND STREET: From left**: scallop shell, shower-curtain hook, toy ring in plastic bubble from vending machine, tire pressure gauge, popcorn, eggcup, dominoes, checkerboard, lollipop, Oreo cookie, dime, ceramic napkin ring, meat thermometer, nickel, ice cream cone, dress pattern (roadway), photographic slide (grating in road). **Figures in foreground**: white seashell, peanut.

General Store

☞ *156 Look-Alikes*

Note: This scene contains many dollhouse miniatures and decorative ceramic beads (not counted as look-alikes).

CEILING AND HANGING FROM CEILING: Playing cards, belt buckles, pull chain, sink plugs, key ring, tiny padlocks, large nail, safety pins, nutcracker, curtain hook*, sea urchin spine (far left salami), cigar ring (on second salami), tiny key on chain, tea ball, manicure scissors, hair clip, tea bags, lace, yardstick, pennies, key chain with metal tag. **BACK WALL: Doorway and window**: pretzels, white birthday candle (doorway window shade), photographic slides, plastic sleeve for slides, waistband hook (doorknob), pearl earrings, chopsticks, brown cigarettes, pocket comb, green Life Saver candy, swizzle stick, burnt matches, crystal decanter stopper*. **In front of door and window**: crossword puzzle, dice, cigar holder, bottle cap, bolt, small comb, melba toast, chess pieces. **Outside door and window**: peppermint stick*, meat thermometer*. **Shelf units**: pen nibs, pencils, (more chopsticks), clear ballpoint pens, crayon boxes, fever thermometer, scallop shell. **Shelves behind shopkeeper**: white chess rook, peppermint candy, toothpaste tube caps, pencil sharpeners, ballpoint pen refill, black sink plug, thimbles, fuse, whistle, roll of film. **Shelves behind deli case**: clear suction cup, cuff link, automobile cigarette lighter, brooch pin-back, electrical connectors, fruit candy in wrapper, red checker, cap-gun cap rolls, screw anchors, tiddlywinks*, caramel, salt and pepper shakers. **Remaining shelves**: gum erasers, sugar cubes, crochet hook, hook (hook-and-eye type), wrapped sticks of gum, bingo call numbers, bubble gum (wrapped and unwrapped), leather wallet, subway token, battery, snap, hose clamp, alligator clip, film cartridge, jack (from game of jacks), pocket screwdriver, hook (scissors), Mary Jane candies, bouillon cubes, toy bullets, pocket aspirin box, spools of thread, model paint can*, mousetrap, tiny lightbulb, single-edge razor blades (wrapped and unwrapped), more snaps, Monopoly hotel, Life Saver candies, liquor bottle cap, Scrabble tile, wafer cookies. COUNTER AREA: Lipstick, button (atop lipstick)*, package carrying handle, picture hook, matchbook, overalls buckle, luggage tags. **Deli case**: hinge, shelled peanuts, garter hook, silver coin*, white electrical wire*, light switch plate, expandable watchband, fuses, crayons, pastels, pink pencil-tip eraser, pebble, stamp moistening jar, hook (tongs). **RIGHT-HAND DISPLAY TABLES AND STOVE**: Rubber stamps, aspirins (soap), postage stamp, dollar bill, hand grenade, buckles, felt-tip marker, cinnamon sticks, rubber band, tin-can lid*, binder clip, drawer pull. **FOREGROUND DISPLAYS AND MERCHANDISE**: Checkerboards (floor). **Counter and basket on left**: fake fingernails, shoelaces*, starfish. **Vacuum cleaner display**: spiral seashell (vase), egg timer, disposable razor, tube of paint, toenail clipper, bulldog paper clip. **Food table and sacks**: drill chuck, key, wooden beads (cheeses), champagne cork cage, pistachio nuts, beer coaster, peanuts, brass paper fastener, clothing label.

PARK AND ZOO

☞ 174 Look-Alikes

BUILDINGS IN BACKGROUND: **Mosque:** coin-roll wrappers, flower bulb, jingle bell*, carpenter's crayon, onion, striped birthday candle, Hershey's Hug candy. **Green-domed building:** votive candle, Scrabble tiles, dollar bill. **Skyscraper:** ballpoint pen and holder. **Red-roofed building:** pushpins, inflator needle (for blowing up balls, etc.), pen nibs, Christmas lights, three-year checkbook calendar. **Church:** bullets, jack (from game of jacks), watchband, graham cracker. **Remaining buildings:** talcum-powder tin, alphabet blocks, felt-tip marker, dice, green pencil-tip eraser, gum erasers, Monopoly house, baseball-game ticket, fine-line marker, discount theater ticket voucher, little cardboard box*. **MIDDLE AREA, LEFT-HAND SIDE:** Broccoli, miniature rolling pin, cigar box, combs, maze puzzle, pastels, pretzels, swizzle sticks, package carrying handle, cinnamon stick*. **Lamppost:** acorn cap, marble, lipstick brush, foreign coin. **Stairway and park:** bread cubes, dominoes, penguin sponge, handbag, chocolate squares, brussels sprout. **PLAYGROUND:** **Boat pond and tower:** tortilla chip, Lucite artist's palette, birdseed bell, toilet paper tube, poppy seeds (gravel). **Drinking fountain:** scallop shell, rhinestone earring, chess bishop, foreign coin*, dog treats. **Sandbox and contents:** tambourine, cork, spool of blue thread, green plastic thimble, diaper pin, animal cracker, starfish, bread crumbs (sand). **Monkey bars:** Ping-Pong paddle, hair bands, wooden matches, hoop earrings. **Base of tree near swings:** checkers*, hairpins*. **Swings:** paintbrush, garter hook, pencils, green birthday candles, paper clips, acorn, wine cork, pistachio nut, dog biscuits, chess knight, blue book. **Clown slide:** game piece (hat), terry ponytail cinch (hat frill), vegetable peeler, magnet, paper clamps, candy cake decorations, shoehorn, paddle-ball toy. **Fence area:** wooden coat hangers, bobby pins, black crayons, drill bits, kidney beans. **Lamppost:** Christmas ornament, brass doorknob, champagne cork cage. **Bench and squirrel:** melba toast, wall hooks, pussy willow catkin, chocolate cookie (drain cover). **ZOO:** Basket. **Antelope and its house:** red pick-up stick, wallet, candy corn, corn kernels, spotted spiral seashell, Brazil nuts. **Ostrich and its pen:** fan-shaped brush, rubber bands, clothespins, wooden combs, pale blue egg. **Birdcage and its inhabitants:** miniature paper umbrella, almond in its shell, coffee bean*, burnt paper matches*, hooks (hook-and-eye type)*, pinecone*, salted sunflower seeds*. **Tree:** pineapple top. **Giraffe:** rubber fingertip, alphabet noodles*, more corn kernels, grain of rice (eyelid), piece of twine, jigsaw puzzle pieces. **Gate:** windshield wiper, wristwatch band, black buttons, sewing machine bobbin, black chess pawns, embroidery scissors, drafting compasses with pencils, fine-point pens, striped sunflower seed. **IN THE PATHWAY:** **Gazebo:** badminton shuttlecock, cigarettes. **Tree:** brown leather glove. **Lamppost:** black chess pawn, toy ring in plastic bubble from vending machine, ballpoint pen with cap, doorbell. **Ice cream vendor, his cart, and customers:** key-chain clasps (his coin holder)*, nail, diaper pins, single-edge razor blades, tapestry sewing needle, chafing-dish candle, supermarket bonus stamp, metal thimble, tiny padlock, dried maple-seed case (girl's ponytail). **Bicycle:** eyelash curler, magnifying glass, snaps. **Fountain, plaza, and angel:** acorn, screw, dried maple-seed case (angel's sleeve), seashell, fuse, drinking glass, hose nozzle, juicer, crystal ashtray, pretzels, popcorn, black-eyed peas, pennies, (more poppy seeds).

AMUSEMENT PARK

☞ 119 Look-Alikes

CASTLE: Tiny darts, ice cream cones (two types), toy trumpet Christmas ornament, brass hose nozzle, spool of red thread, tiny stud earrings, swizzle stick (flagpole)*, penny, plastic squeeze bottle, white dominoes, honey dipper, plastic nozzle, clothespins, pink pencil-tip erasers, striped wallet, chess bishop, coin-roll wrapper, party horn, magnet, book, broccoli, pearl earring. **FOUNTAIN:** Baby teething ring*, Christmas lights, paintbrushes, spiral seashell. **RIDES IN BACKGROUND:** **Ferris wheel:** scissors, binder clips, embroidery hoops, hair perming rods, yellow plastic cocktail forks*, pick-up sticks, pencil sharpener, garden fork, pocket comb, Afro picks. **Roller coaster:** guitar, toothpicks. **Moon shot:** cake decorator, takeout coffee-cup lid. **Dragon and its ticket booth:** clamp, drafting compass, pliers, autumn oak leaves, miniature paper umbrella, tiny buckle. **"Wild West" exhibit:** postage stamps. **Smaller wheel on right:** dartboard, nutcracker, black dominoes*. **RIDES AND ATTRACTIONS IN MIDDLE DISTANCE:** **Carousel:** bell, toy crown, jam jar, peanuts (horses), bicycle sprocket. **Kiosk:** jingle bell,

red stick for homemade Popsicle. **Ticket booth**: cupcake paper, another tiny buckle, rubber band*. **Daffy Discs**: pencils, suction-cup dart, silk daffodils, big red buttons, 45 record, Frisbee*, plastic sword toothpicks. **Balloon vendor**: ball-headed straight pins. **Topsy Turvy**: spinning top, tubes of paint, guitar picks, sequins (propellers), bobby pins, gold necklace. **Circular ride behind boy**: tambourine, juicer, keys, retractable tape measure*. **BOY ON RIDE:** Silk autumn maple leaf, twirler's baton, suitcase. BOOTHS AND STRUCTURES IN FOREGROUND: **Game booths**: knitting needle, cap-gun caps, Chinese finger puzzle, more peanuts (teddy bears), thimble, pearls, chess pawns, tickets, cigarette lighters, (Note: Guatemalan "worry dolls" are miniatures rather than look-alikes), fishhooks, crayon. **Cotton candy booth**: yellow pencil-tip eraser, tiny toy rabbit, spotted seashell, tip of crayon, nailbrush, price tag, photographic slide holder, chewing gum in wrapper*, cotton swabs, pink eraser, votive candle. **Children's ball jump**: sink plug, billiard ball, pot holder weaving loom, rolls of streamers, parakeet perch with bells, pearl anklet, jelly beans. **Behind ball jump**: tire pressure gauges, combs, pretzel sticks, spiral notepad. **"Test Your Strength"**: meat thermometer, playing cards*, lid of 1% milk bottle. **On ground**: leather glove, spices.

HOTEL

☞ 129 Look-Alikes

TOP OF WALL: Spool of thread*, wooden spoons, cardboard matches, accordion peg coatrack, unbleached coffee filters, wine cork, pretzels, yardsticks, folding knives (archway on right). SHOP WALL ON LEFT: Five-dollar bill, jigsaw puzzle pieces, doorstop, plastic spiders, cigarillos, brass letter *T*, bubble wrap, small screwdriver, tiny buckle (doorknob plate)* (Note: Tiny bottle is a miniature rather than a look-alike), playing card, spiral seashell, golf tee. **BACK WALL:** Chocolate bars, crayons. **Marble pillars**: buttons, map sections, rubber bands*, sandwich cookies. **Arch**: fancy hair clip. **Sculpture on wall**: polished pebble, beige chess pawns, spiral cookies, corn kernel, night-light fixture, *biscotto* cookie. **On stairway wall**: feather fishing lure, stone arrowhead, embroidery hoop, artificial leaf, shade pull, pencils. **On upper landing wall**: tea ball, metal bookend, kitty litter scoop, squishy fish fishing lure, cup hook, pinecone*. **RESTAURANT:** Lace fan, white nylon gloves, six-pack plastic rings, toy green plastic dinosaurs, crystal doorknob, toilet plunger, small wooden scoop, hairpins, cupcake papers, tiny artificial flowers (lampshades)*, brass paper fasteners (vases)*, acorn (chicken), thimble, nailbrush. OBJECTS IN FRONT OF BACK WALL: Razor, crossword puzzle, bullets, gold-toned coins*, meat thermometer, hoop earring, hose nozzle, comb, graham crackers, rubber stamp, Christmas ball, chess knight, jumbo sidewalk chalk, wooden crochet hook, plastic cocktail forks, shaving brush, ivory-colored dominoes. **HANGING LAMPS:** Ballpoint pen with top, doorbell, votive candle, bicycle sprocket, silk flowers. LOUNGE AREA: Pennies, pen nib, peat pot, tiny gold safety pins, penknife, pea pods, ceramic napkin ring, coin purse, bobby pins (on front of chair arms)*, restaurant coffee creamer, saltshaker, shoe-polish tin, lamp socket, orange suede gloves, postage stamps, picture frame, spool of gold thread, gold-foil-wrapped chocolate coin, bars of soap (two sizes), camouflage cloth, autumn leaves, dried maple-seed cases, doilies, red and natural pistachio nuts, feathers.

RECEPTION AND ELEVATOR AREA: Silver pepper mill, lavendar ponytail elastic*, black chess pawn, oven thermometer, old-fashioned key, museum admission tag, marble-based desk pen set, peacock feather*, leather wallet, chopsticks, unopened tube of flypaper, dog chews, toggle buttons, nutmeg grater, plastic protractor, window lock, clear ballpoint pen, table knives, silver crochet hook, wooden switch plate, single-edge razor blades, card of thumbtacks.

NEIGHBORHOOD

☞ 98 Look-Alikes

PHARMACY BUILDING: Crackers, folding carpenter's ruler, dollar bill, paintbrushes, candle, electrical plug, sunglasses, postage stamp, worry doll, single-edge razor blade*, white button, plastic skull, Smarties candy*, stick of gum in wrapper*, toothbrushes, ballpoint pens, dental floss container*, card of thumbtacks. JUANITA'S BODEGA BUILDING: Pistachio nuts, dog biscuits (two sizes), wooden matches, hoop earring, corrugated cardboard, thimble, rubber stamp*, yellow stick for homemade Popsicle (lamp), Goldfish crackers, corn kernels, taco shell, sugar birthday cake letters, birthday candles, corncob holders, tape measure, plastic protractor, pretzel, package carrying handle, pencils, orange button (door-knob), picture hook, diaper pin, bottle of pickled chilies, part of wallet (door)*, miniature watercolor set, wristwatch, seashell, party blow-out toy, yellow button, (another worry doll), Cheerio, red electrical connector, embroidery floss, cranberries, popcorn, clothespins, audiocassette, postage stamp, Chiclets gum, number puzzle. **PARK AREA:** Kale, broccoli, package wrapped in gray paper and white string, book, flat-leaf parsley*, pretzel sticks, saltshaker, white chalk, wooden blocks, popcorn, crayons, needle-nose pliers, key, ballpoint pen refill, stick of gum in wrapper, cut pencils. MURAL AND SKYSCRAPER: Jigsaw puzzle piece, pink glove, skeleton emblem, graph paper. **BAKERY BUILDING:** Kidney beans, melba toasts, plaid shoelace, ruler, cap-gun caps, drafting compass, red shoelace*, tan chess pawn*, baby-bottle nipple, clear plastic change purse, pistachio nuts, penny, bar of soap, birthday candles. **SIDEWALK AREA:** Slices of bread, tortilla chip, baby pacifiers, bulldog paper clips*, blue drinking straw, screwdriver, olive with pimento.

SWEET SHOP

☛ *117 Look-Alikes*

CEILING AND WALLS: Dollar bills, takeout coffee-cup lids, baby-bottle nipples, shade pull, plastic cocktail forks, playing cards, kitty litter scoops, small old-fashioned key, restaurant order pads, drinking straws, button, sword toothpicks. **BOOTH AREA:** Books, saltshaker (lamp), paintbrushes, lanyard clasps, acorn cap, Afro picks, fig bars, pocket calculator, toenail clipper, supermarket bonus stamp, electronic connectors (vases), cigar holder, bottle cap, fishhook, number puzzle, travel checkerboard. **Jukebox:** toy pilot's wings, plastic protractor, whistle, button*, cold caplets in wrapper, pencils, egg slicer. **Small cabinet:** barrette, birthday candles, tiny light bulbs, matchboxes, corn kernels, clothespins, safety pins, toy car, gum erasers. SODA FOUNTAIN, BEHIND THE COUNTER: Wooden clothes hanger, pennies, old-fashioned key, scallop shell, toy compass, bottle stoppers, penknife, chopsticks, yardstick, chess pawns, package carrying handles, cigarillos, ballpoint pens, compact discs, drop earring, night-light fixture, guitar finger pick, postage stamps, clear pushpins, anchovy tin*, orange crayon, bells, bottle cap, spark plug, thimble, bamboo beads, bingo call number, luggage tag, coin changer, harmonica, fuse, fondue fork (towel rack)*. **COUNTER AREA:** Bouillon cube, wedding band, matchbook, overalls buckle, wooden matches, red and yellow crayon tips, pencil sharpeners, two small padlocks, tiny spiral seashells, birthday-candle holder, blue magnifying glass (pie plate)*, buttons (pie)*, retractable measuring tape, ballpoint pen refills, cocktail forks, another old-fashioned key, unwrapped sticks of gum, blue knitting needle, dried apricots, silver dollars, brass hose nozzles, coffee beans (girl's ponytails). **FOREGROUND:** LP record, dominoes, pretzels, pretzel sticks, round crackers, tea-tin lids, baby-bottle nipples, garter hook, digital clock, pen nibs, clear change purse, leather wallet, tapestry sewing needle, crochet hook, powder puff (left-hand cake), pan of watercolor paint, white poker chip (middle cake plate)*, party streamer roll, six-inch clear plastic ruler.

CIRCUS

☛ *113 Look-Alikes*

TENT: Trenchcoat, pair of pants, large zipper (on right), American flag (partly behind band), small plastic bandage, paper doll outfit, fishhook with lure, silver evening purse*, pearl sweater clasp. **TENTPOLES, RIGGING, AND LIGHTS: Up high, left to right:** drafting compasses with pencils, garter hook, TV antenna, red and blue valve handles, arrows, two skirt hangers, covered hook-and-eye, alligator clips*, knitting needles, hoop earrings*, large bobby pin, safety pins, lanyard clasp, beaded chain (aerialist's ladder), carpenter's clamp, beaded necklace (aerialist's rope), domino, door latch hook, drop earring, sewing needle, cheese slicer, yardstick (tentpole, right foreground). **Trapezes:** cord necklace with pendant, barrette, eyeglass strap, cotton swab. **Lower down, left to right:** bulldog paper clips, key holder, keys, artist's paintbrush, silver pencil sharpener, bike reflector, pencils, fishhook and lure, chopsticks, gold-edged ribbon (ladder), brass paper fasteners, corncob holders, M&M's, faucet aerator, vegetable peeler, blue pencil-tip erasers, billiard cue chalk, toy googly-eyes, aspirins, (another fishhook and lure), hook (hook-and-eye type), binder clips. **Technician's platform**: pushpins, wristwatch face, blue pet halter, bottle cap, roll of film, paper clamp*, track for model train. SURROUNDING THE RING: Striped birthday candles, alphabet stencils, audiocassette, matchboxes, wooden matches. **Band**: paper fastener box, eye shadow applicator, spools of thread. **Entranceway**: model train boxcar, party blow-out toys, star-shaped candleholder, small yellow candle, peacock feathers, tiny gold safety pins, dollar bill (rug). **Calliope**: toy flutes, protractor, pen nibs, flagpole finial*, toy bullet, old-fashioned key, yellow paper clips, corn kernels, penny, harmonica, binder clip (hitch). **RING AREA AND PERFORMERS**: **Animal stands**: cat toy, cupcake paper, rubber band, hosiery garter, wooden block (far right). **Ring**: tickets, cap-gun caps, straw place mat, patchwork hot pad, champagne cork cages. **Baby carriage**: miniature cheese, hook (hook-and-eye type), green buttons. **Springboard**: artist's sandpaper pad, silver snap. **Floor**: silk scarf, paper bags. **Clown**: tiny spiral seashell, ponytail holder, tubes of paint. **Aerialist**: fake fingernails. **Harlequin girl**: terry ponytail cinch, purple silk flower, garlic cloves.

HARBOR

☞ *113 Look-Alikes*

BACKGROUND BUILDINGS: Fancy canister. **Brown building**: whisk broom, clipboard, brown crayons, fondue forks, quarter, cigarillos. **In front of brown building**: bricks, jumbo sidewalk chalk, talcum-powder tin, felt-tip pen cap, wooden comb, chess king, alphabet block. **Dark green building**: cow bell, insulated staples, book. **To right of dark green building**: folding carpenter's ruler, level, blackboard eraser, striped wallet, CD boxes, rubber stamp, pocket calculator, fig bars, egg slicer, address book with pencil, silver thimble, size/price tag, felt-tip marker, (more alphabet blocks). WATERFRONT STRUCTURES: **Left-hand loading dock**: mailbox (with red flag partly raised), graham crackers, red zipper pull, cup hook, X-Acto knife, finishing nail, drop earring, drafting compass with pencil, pepper packets, toy giraffe, tiny snaps, cap-gun caps, unwrapped cough drops, unwrapped sticks of gum, cutting board with built-in knife, cinnamon sticks. **Gray loading dock**: penny, pencil, wrapped sesame candy, matchbox, small black button. **Ferry building and dock**: pliers, disposable razors, toy compass, cuff link, tape measure. **Gas storage tank**: sugar shaker, admission ticket. **Buildings near ocean liner**: pocket aspirin box, toy baby bottle, gum eraser, battery, audiocassette, artist's sandpaper pad (pier), green party noisemaker, steel hinges. **BRIDGE AND SUPPORTS**: Brown plastic doorstop, nutcrackers, windshield wipers. FAR SHORE: Natural sponges, matchbook, pencil sharpener, blue birthday candle, dominoes, plastic lizard. **BOATS**: **Boat docked at left**: canned ham, brass paper fastener*, sewing machine bobbin with red thread, wing nut. **Docked cargo ship**: nail clipper, bottle cap, pistachio shells, drafting compass, crochet hook, spool of white thread, lipstick, old-fashioned towel rack, sewing machine bobbin (on mast), heel protector*. **Ferry**: nailbrush, scrub brush. **Ocean liner**: steam iron, dice, white domino, disposable lighters, key*, white pushpin, upside-down miniature figure. **Ship under bridge**: bottle/can opener. **Sailboat**: guitar pick, sewing needle*. **Tugboat**: doll shoe, inflator needle. **Departing ship in foreground**: mandolin, Life Saver candy, burnt matches, black chess pawn, doorstop, wooden coat hanger, cigarettes. **WATER**: Blue lace, white lace, cut-off crayons (buoys).

∽